# MINEHEAD, DUNSTER &
# IN
# OLD PRINTS

A collection of etchings with commentary

by

W. H. (BEN) NORMAN

Published by W. H. (Ben) Norman
Lyn Cottage, Mill Lane, Watchet TA23 0AR

£2

© First Published 1995

ISBN  09510842 - 2 - 4

All rights reserved

Printed by Williton Printers,
5 Long Street, Williton,
Taunton, Somerset TA4 4QN.
Tel. 01984 632731

## ACKNOWLEDGEMENTS

Acknowledgements and thanks to my family and friends and especially to
Mr. David Bromwich of the Somerset Local History Library

**DEDICATION**

**To my grandchildren**

**RUBY, JACK AND SALLY**

# CONTENTS

Minehead.............................................................................Pages 1 to 12

Cleeve Abbey ....................................................................Pages 13 to 14

Dunster ..............................................................................Pages 15 to 20

St. Audries..........................................................................Pages 21 to 24

Watchet and Brendon Hill....................................................Pages 25 to 36

Combe Sydenham ..............................................................Pages 37 to 39

# INTRODUCTION

Picture postcards giving views of a town or village have been popular since the early 1900s. Before postcards became available, however, little engravings of local views were produced and sold at 'fancy goods' shops in each locality. Usually in booklet form they were purchased by holiday makers to keep as mementos of their visit. Today they are collectors' items and much sought after.

Although not as accurate as photographic views, these delightful little pictures illustrated the various locations and way of life as it appeared at that time. Historically the engravings are important, for often they provide pictorial records of interesting old structures long since altered, fallen into decay or demolished. The reproduction of some of them in this book allow us to peep into the past and to appreciate the old world charm of West Somerset in bygone years.

Most of these etchings date from between 1850-80, but two much earlier local views by the famous artist J. M. W. Turner, R.A., have been included, as well as an even older view of Combe Sydenham dated 1783.

Ancient buildings and particularly old Harbour Towns invariably induce quaint old legends or sayings. Some are mentioned in this book.

## MINEHEAD AND DUNSTER CASTLE

During the early 1800s the renowned artist J. M. W. Turner, R.A., travelled extensively sketching and painting scenic settings which impressed him. In particular he enjoyed coastal aspects.
This is one of many views by Turner, engraved by Cooke in 1821 and included in a series entitled 'Picturesque Views on the Southern Coast of England'. Turner's viewpoint for this picture was probably from the rising ground above Blue Anchor Inn. His original water-colour of the scene hangs in the Lady Lever Gallery at Port Sunlight.

*Minehead and Dunster Castle*

2

# MINEHEAD CHURCH FROM THE HIGHER TOWN

The Parish Church of St. Michael stands in a prominent position above the town.
Built in the fifteenth century it has a beautifully ornate screen dividing the Chancel
from the Nave.
It is believed that from a window in the turret a light was kept burning to help
guide ships and local fishing boats towards the harbour.
The 87ft tower contains a clock and a peal of ten bells. According to old Quay-
Town fishermen, the bells chime out the message:
"Herrings and Bread, go the Bells of Minehead."
Today there are ample supplies of bread in the town, but regrettably the once
plentiful shoals of herring are few and far between.

*Minehead Church from the Higher Town*

4

## MINEHEAD, Somersetshire

This pretty little sketch of Bampton Street, with the Parish Church and North Hill in the background, is a gem.

The artist captured the scene as it was in 1853. Remarkably the aspect has not altered beyond recognition and it is interesting today to visit Bampton Street and in one's mind to imagine it clear of traffic. The picturesque thatched cottages and much of the charm of one of Minehead's oldest streets can still be seen and enjoyed.

*Minehead, Somerset*

6

## VIEW OF THE PARADE FROM WATER LANE

The tall building (centre) is the 'Plume of Feathers', an old coaching inn and a building of great character and charm. It catered for many early visitors to Minehead.

Regrettably it was demolished in 1966 and its space was developed for modern shops, showrooms and also a night club.

The building on the right with the central clock turret contained the old Fish Market. It was knocked down in 1902 for road widening and the erection of a larger Market House.

The little gate and turnstile in the foreground gave access to a muddy track known as Water Lane.

Prior to the 1870s Water Lane, with an open stream beside it, led from a bridge near the Old Priory building to the sea. This stream now runs in a culvert beneath the road which today is known as The Avenue. The outfall of the stream can still be seen from the beach.

*Parade, Minehead from Water Lane*

8

# MINEHEAD, NORTH HILL & QUAY TOWN

This view of Minehead's sea front, with the Harbour in the background, is dated 1853, some years before the Railway brought the main influx of day trippers and visitors to the town.

No houses can be seen on North Hill and hardly any sea-front buildings apart from the Quay Town cottages existed at that time. The scene was to change dramatically in the following 21 years.

Many and varied are the tales of an old Minehead woman known as 'Old Mother Leakey'. It was claimed she often reappeared in ghostly form after her death in 1634. Usually at night she would haunt and terrify her former neighbours in Quay Street and was believed by old mariners to have caused several shipwrecks by 'whistling up' gale force winds.
They complained that during one of their May Day celebrations, a sudden manifestation by Old Mother Leakey had terrified their hobby horse at White Cross Lane.
The horse had then bolted back to its stable in Quay Street. "He did bide there all day, shaking like a leaf, and affeared to come out," they lamented. The old woman's haunting was eventually brought to an end after investigation by the Bishop of Bath and Wells, followed by the 'Bell, Book and Candle' treatment of a local clergyman.

*Minehead from the sea*

## *MINEHEAD BEACH*

Dated 1878, this picture strikingly illustrates the rapid advance of Minehead's tourist industry which followed the arrival of the Railway in 1874.
Two commodious hotels can be seen on the sea front. One of them, the luxurious Hotel Metropole, was opened in 1875. Top-hatted gentry with the ladies attired in long crinoline dresses parade along the sea-front — taking the air.
Boating activity in the bay is apparent. At that time sea bathing was already quite popular, but 'mixed bathing' was very much disapproved of. Puritanical attitudes insisted that separate sections of beaches be reserved for ladies only. A couple of bathing machines can be seen at the water's edge. These enabled ladies to change into voluminous bathing costumes and to enter the water without shocking any member of the opposite sex who happened to look their way!

*Minehead Beach*

# CLEEVE ABBEY

Cleeve Abbey was founded in 1188 for Cistercian Monks by William de Romara and dedicated to 'Our Blessed Lady of the Cliff'. The pious Brothers at no time numbered more than 28. They alluded to the pleasant valley in which their Abbey stood as 'The Valley of Flowers'.

After the Dissolution in 1536 the Abbey Church, adjacent to the cloister, was razed to the ground. There is a legend, however, that before the last Abbot went away in 1539, he buried plate and other treasures in the ground!

Fortunately many of the Monastic buildings were not demolished, but were used to store fodder and to house farm animals, etc. This continued to be so until the property came into the hands of the late Mr. Geoffrey Luttrell in 1895.

Within a very short time the buildings were cleared and the animals driven out. All the remaining structures of this local Ecclesiastical treasure were destined to be preserved for posterity. Today Cleeve Abbey is cherished and looked after by 'English Heritage'.

There is a discerning inscription in Latin above the Gatehouse which, translated, reads 'Gate be open — shut to no honest person'.

The Abbey is close to and well sign-posted from Washford on the A39 road between Williton and Minehead.

It is open to the public and well worth a visit.

*Cleeve Abbey*

14

# DUNSTER CASTLE

Dunster was granted to William de Mohun shortly after the Norman Invasion of England in 1066. Lady Elizabeth Luttrell bought the reversion in 1376 and it remained in the Luttrell family's possession for 600 years.

The Castle has been structurally altered at various times and seen the ebb and flow of many a battle. It was besieged during the Civil War by Colonel Robert Blake. After 160 days of unrelenting attack, the Royalist Colonel Francis Wyndham and his brave defending soldiers were forced to surrender — but with honour.

During the Monmouth rebellion in 1688 the local militia supported William of Orange. Later, under the command of Colonel Francis Luttrell, they formed the nucleus of the famous Green Howard Regiment.

In 1976 the Castle and its Park was given to the National Trust by Lt. Colonel Walter Luttrell, MC.

Now open to the public, it is a delightful and most interesting place to visit. This etching gives a pleasing view of the Castle with the little River Avill flowing through the parkland below.

The parish church of St. George in the background is said to be the finest in Somerset.

*Dunster Castle*

16

# *DUNSTER YARN MARKET AND HIGH STREET*

The picturesque village of Dunster attracts more visitors than any other in West Somerset.

This scene of the yarn market and castle beyond has delighted countless artists and photographers.

The hexagonal shaped building was constructed in the early 1600's by George Luttrell for the sale of wool and woollen cloth. The manufacture of woollen fabric was a major industry in the area years ago.

During the Civil War C-1645, the building was badly damaged, a hole made by a cannon ball can still be seen in one of the roofing beams.

As well as the Church, Castle and Yarn Market the village has many other interesting old buildings. They include a working (water powered) corn mill, a Pack Horse Bridge, a circular Dovecote and a quaint old building known as The Nunnery.

In a beautiful setting in Exmoor National Park, Dunster is a village that merits careful preservation.

*Dunster Yarn Market and High Street*

18

# THE RUINS ON CONYGAR HILL

The majority of people who pass through West Somerset will have noticed the battlements of Conygar Tower perched on a hill beside the A39 road at Dunster. Protruding above the surrounding trees it can be seen for many miles and adds a little mystery to the rural landscape.

The tower was constructed as a folly in 1775 by Henry Fownes Luttrell. At the same time he constructed the ruined gatehouse — shown in the picture. These ruins are situated a little to the west of the tower and because of surrounding trees cannot be seen from any distance.

When the artist sketched this picture in the 1870s the trees were not so dense and he had a good view of Minehead through the archway.

*Minehead from Conygar*

20

# ST AUDRIES HOUSE

St. Audries House is situated at the western end of the Quantock Hills. It stands in an idyllic wooded valley sloping down to the sea-shore. Here, a spectacular waterfall cascades over the cliff. At one time at this point one could enter into an exciting grotto specially built, and lined with ammonites and other fossils. It had a little window in the edge of the cliff overlooking the sea. A more spectacular grotto lined with sea shells was constructed in the grounds nearer the house. The Manor of St. Audries (or West Quantoxhead) is recorded in the Domesday Book in 1086 and has changed hands many times. In 1835 it was purchased by Sir Peregrine Fuller-Palmer-Acland for his daughter Isabel. She was the wife-to-be of Sir Alexander Acland Hood, Bart., and they lived there after their marriage in 1848. Their grandson, Alexander Peregrine Acland Hood, Bart. (the second Lord St. Audries), sold the whole estate in 1925.

The house and part of the parkland eventually passed to the Misses Townsend who developed it in 1934 into a boarding school for girls. This enterprise came to an end in 1991. The house and grounds are at present in the hands of caretakers and not open to the public.

This delightful and rare view of St. Audries House illustrates how it appeared in 1865. Five years later the mansion was largely rebuilt and altered drastically under the guidance of London architect John Norton. It then provided 42 bedrooms. A coal gas works was built in the grounds to provide heating and lighting for the mansion. Coal for the gas works was brought from Wales by sea, to St. Audries beach, and carted up the slipway to the works.

The little sailing vessel which brought the coal from Cardiff, was the 'Tom' a forty ton smack. It was commanded by Capt. William Norman (Grandfather of the writer.)

*St. Audries House*

22

## ST. ETHELDREDA'S CHURCH, WEST QUANTOXHEAD

The Parish Church of West Quantoxhead (St. Audries) is dedicated to St. Etheldreda. It was erected at great expense in 1856 by Sir Alexander Acland Hood, Bart., to the design of John Norton — a London architect. It replaced a much older Church which stood closer to St. Audries House.

The interior of the Church is handsome; its arches being supported by polished columns of monolithic Babbacombe marble.

Externally the building is pleasing with a square tower and turret, surmounted by a graceful spire. Almost surrounded by a pinewood forest, it would be difficult to find a more picturesque setting for a Church. It comes suddenly and delightfully into the view of travellers passing along the A39 road from Williton towards Kilve.

*St. Audries Church, West Quantockhead*

24

## WATCHET, Somersetshire

This view of Watchet Harbour was depicted by the artist J. M. W. Turner, R.A., and engraved by George Cooke in the year 1820. It forms part of a series entitled: 'Picturesque Views of the Southern Coast of England'.

Only 23 years earlier, the famous poet Samuel Taylor Coleridge, while visiting Watchet, was inspired to write his masterpiece 'The Rime of the Ancient Mariner'. The whereabouts of Turner's original water colour of Watchet Harbour is unknown. Another famous visitor after inspecting the harbour in 1724 was rather critical of its construction.  He considered it was not built high enough to give adequate protection to ships.  This fault finder was none other than Daniel Defoe the renowned author of Robinson Crusoe.  When shown ammonites and other fossils on the foreshore however, he confessed he was completely mystified, he had no knowledge as to their origin.  Indeed at that time, neither did anyone else in the country.

*Watchet*

26

# ST. DECUMAN'S CHURCH, WATCHET

Situated on a hill above the town, this beautiful old Church is mainly of perpendicular architecture with Early English work in the Chancel. It is considered by many to be among the finest in Somerset, and one of which some hair-raising legends are told:

1) The church was named after a Celtic missionary, one 'Decuman'. In the fifth century he reputedly sailed from Wales to Watchet on a raft accompanied by a cow. His efforts to convert the local heathen by preaching were interrupted by a wicked fellow. This local man, irritated possibly by Decuman's unfamiliar accent, chopped off his head with a hatchet.

Unperturbed, Decuman calmly replaced his severed head onto his body and carried on with his good work. Deservedly he was made a Saint and the Church was later named after him.

2) Another gruesome tale handed down from the 16th century is of an evil sexton. This misguided man attempted at night to steal a tight fitting wedding ring from the newly interred body of Lady Florence Wyndham, which lay in a vault in the Church.

As he hacked at her finger with a knife, the lady awoke from what proved to be a death-like trance. The sexton fled in terror and was never seen again but Lady Wyndham returned to her home at Kentsford. Her subsequent offspring continue the Wyndham lineage to this day.

*St. Decuman's Church, Watchet*

28

# BRENDON HILL INCLINE ON THE
# WEST SOMERSET MINERAL RAILWAY

Following the discovery of iron ore deposits on the Brendon Hills, a substantial mining industry was set up in 1855. Its purpose was to supply this mineral in substantial quantities to the large smelting works at Ebbw Vale in South Wales.

Over 300 miners were employed and two new villages built on the hills to accommodate them and their families. A church and two chapels were established for their spiritual guidance.

A ten mile railway was constructed to transport the ore to the nearest port of Watchet where it was shipped across the Bristol Channel to South Wales.

A massive incline had to be built to enable the railway trucks loaded with ore from the hill-top mines to be lowered 800ft down the steep hillside. This incline, with a gradient of 1 in 4 and with winding gear at the top, was considered a great engineering feat at that time.

For some years the hills and villages of West Somerset reverberated to the clatter of the mining industry. Hundreds of thousands of tons of ore were mined and shipped away.

The whole enterprise eventually came to an end when it was unable to compete with much cheaper iron ore imported from Spain.

The last ore was mined in 1910 and the railway lines taken up in 1917.

A working model of the incline and interesting artefacts from the mines, mineral railway, and harbour can be seen at Watchet Market House Museum. Also on display are fossils, Stone Age implements, and coins from Watchet's Saxon mint. Situated near the harbour slipway, the Museum opens daily during the summer. Thanks to voluntary staff, entrance charges are minimal.

*Brendon Hill incline on the West Somerset Mineral Railway*

30

## WATCHET HARBOUR, Somersetshire

During the 1860s Watchet was a hive of activity. As well as its busy foundry, flour and paper mills, its harbour was very active and greatly enlarged to deal with the export of thousands of tons of iron ore.

At that time, Watchet was the terminus for two completely separate railways. Railway No. 1 from the Brendon Hill Iron Ore Mines. Railway No. 2 from the county town of Taunton was a branch of the Bristol and Exeter Railway. Hundreds of day trippers from Taunton as well as 'merry' miners from the Brendon Hills came by train to Watchet. This was their nearest seaside town.

Richard Stoate Date, a local entrepreneur, organised paddle steamer trips to take many of these pleasure-seeking folk to Minehead, which at that time had no railway service.

This picture, dated 25th August, 1864, shows (on the left) one of his little paddle steamers about to leave the harbour. Usually they had a brass band on board! What appears to be a road in the foreground is actually a slipway leading onto the beach. After a few years it was washed away by the sea. An access path was made to the clifftop area overlooking the harbour. This was known as 'The Pleasure Ground' and refreshments could be obtained from a pretty little specially built thatched kiosk (not shown in the picture).

*Watchet Harbour*

32

## *BREAKWATER AND ENTRANCE TO WATCHET HARBOUR*

This delightful little picture dated 1865 illustrates the newly constructed wooden breakwater with its hexagonal cast iron lighthouse at its head.
Projecting into the harbour is the iron ore loading jetty. A steam railway engine can be seen hauling away some empty iron ore trucks.
In the foreground on the East Pier groups of well-dressed people are probably awaiting the arrival of a pleasure steamer for a cruise to Minehead or Ilfracombe.
A black ball hoisted on the signal mast indicates to the approaching ship that there is sufficient depth of water in the harbour for her to enter. . . . . Happy days.

*Breakwater and entrance to Watchet Harbour*

34

# WATCHET IN THE DAYS OF STEAM, WIND AND HORSE POWER

The Church Tower, the Methodist Church, and the newly built Royal National Lifeboat House (nearest building) can be seen in this etching c.1875.
Those were the days of sailing ships, steam locomotives, and man's great helpmate — the horse.
Six horses were required whenever it was necessary to haul Watchet's lifeboat over the rocky foreshore for a low-water launch. The boat, of the self-righting rowing and sailing type, required a crew of 12 men and 20 launchers. It never lacked volunteers.
After a new motor lifeboat was stationed at nearby Minehead, Watchet's Station was closed in 1944.
No safety railings can be seen on the Esplanade, neither is there a shelter or bandstand. These amenities were added during the early 1900s and were paid for by an enthusiastic fund raising group who organised mud-larks, water sports and sailing regattas, etc.

*Watchet*

36

## COMBE SYDENHAM

This interesting old house and estate is situated near Monksilver at the eastern end of Exmoor National Park.
Known originally as 'Combe' it was held in 1086 by William de Mohun. Late in the fourteenth century and for over three hundred years it was owned by the Sydenhams — hence its present name — Combe Sydenham. Later it was the home of the Notley family. This picture was published in 1783.
Today the historic old house and its grounds, owned by W. A. C. Theed, Esq., is open to the public and much enjoyed by visitors.

*Combe Sydenham*

38

# *The Combe Sydenham Legend*

There is a captivating 16th century legend featuring Sir George Sydenham's daughter, Elizabeth. Seemingly she was very much in love and engaged to marry Sir Francis Drake, the famous circumnavigator of the world. They planned to marry as soon as he returned from his next foray against the Spanish fleet.
Sir George had never really taken to Drake and would have preferred his daughter to marry an interested local wealthy man.

After several years had passed, Drake had not returned from his travels. Sir George, therefore, persuaded Elizabeth that Drake was unlikely ever to return and in all probability was dead. She should, he insisted, marry the local affluent suitor. After much parental pressure Elizabeth reluctantly agreed.
On the set wedding day, fortunately just before she had taken her wedding vows, there was a terrific bang, a blinding flash and a 'cannon ball' hurtled down from the sky. "Gadzooks, what the devil was that?" cried Sir George in great alarm.
"Methinks it's a signal from my Francis", said Elizabeth quite calmly, and she refused point blank to proceed with the wedding. Her intuition was quite right. Drake had returned to Plymouth that very day and he hastened to claim his bride.
It is recorded that they were married in 1585.
As for the cannon ball, it is still there for all to see. There are some people who claim it is a meteorite and not a cannon ball at all.
Be that as it may, it did the trick and the local wealthy man, although quite upset, had no difficulty in finding another bride.